Binary Options:
A Complete Guide on Binary Options Trading

Table of Contents

Introduction

Investing your money is a smart financial move. It is a great way to put your money to work for you and ensures that you are taken care of for the long term. There are many ways that you are able to invest your money depending on the goals that you have present. For example, some people like to invest in the stock market or in real estate and turn their investments into a full time income. Others may want to put some extra money into their retirement plan or a savings account to ensure that they are set when it is time to take it easy later in life.

While all of these and more are great investment opportunities, this guidebook is going to look at binary options. Binary options are a simple process of making a prediction on how well a currency, or other asset, is going to do at some point in the future. Sometimes the length is just a minute and it can expand out to an hour, a day, and even longer. If you are right with your prediction, you can earn a predetermined amount of money. But if you are wrong, you can lose money.

There are a lot of different aspects that come with binary options, despite having a simple premise. There is a high risk factor with this option and you need to understand how the market is going to work both short term and long term. But with a bit of practice and following the ideas that are in this guidebook, binary options can quickly become an investing method that will make you a lot of money.

When you are ready to diversify your portfolio or you are looking for a way to finally put your money to work for you, it is time to read through this guidebook. You are sure to find all the success you are looking for in no time once you understand what binary options are all about and how the market works. So let's get started with investing today!

Chapter 1: What are Binary Options?

When it comes to investing, there are many options you can choose from. Some choose to go into the real estate market and go with one of those options including flipping homes, renting them out, and so much more. Others are more comfortable placing their money into the stock market while others may wan to just take he safe route and place their money in a comfortable savings or retirement plan for down the road. All of these can be great ways to secure your future or make a nice income.

If you are looking into the investment field, one option you should consider is binary options. These investments come in many different names including digital options, fixed return options, and all or nothing options. This kind of investment can be difficult to comprehend as you will not be purchasing or selling an item during the process. Basically, you will be either making or losing money when a currency of some sort, perhaps a currency from another country or even currency from online sources like Bitcoin, starts to change value.

You will never hold that currency in your hands though. You will simply make a prediction about the value of the currency at some point in advance. There are different lengths and times that you can go with, from a few weeks to many years, and then when that time length comes up and you predicted correctly, you can earn a certain percentage, which is determined at the beginning of the investment, on your prediction.

To some people, this can be a little bit scary. You are putting your money on a prediction and have no tangible product to hold onto at the end of the day. Yes, you could make a lot of money, but unlike stocks in a company or gold, you have nothing to hold onto even if the value where to go down. This kind of investing is not for everyone. It takes someone who understands the market, someone who is willing to try out a lot of different strategies, and an idea that is may go wrong the first few times as you learn the market in order to handle this kind of trading.

And this is why binary options can be so rewarding. Lots of people are too worried or scared about losing money in this kind of investment so they choose to go with something else. The market is not saturated and if you are smart about your money, and only bring money to the table that you can afford to lose, this can be a very profitable endeavor.

Who Should Do Binary Options

Binary options can be a great investment choice for a lot of different people. First, if you are looking for a new way to invest your money and you feel that you are good at understanding the market, this can be a good place for you. If you are willing to work on predictions because you know when something is good, or you trust your financial advisor to do this for you, and you are willing to wait months or years before you get a good return back, then this could be the right investment for you.

Those who don't mind waiting out for the best returns and know how to invest their money wisely so they aren't spending money they can't afford to lose, may find that this almost untapped market is a good place to give a try. You also have to be willing to take some risks. You are not always going to be right with your predictions, especially early on in the game as you start to learn the ropes. If losing money, even money you are able to afford to lose, makes you feel nervous, binary options is not the best option for you.

Who Should Avoid Binary Options

Not everyone is going to find that binary options is the best choice for them. Each investment opportunity has its positives and negatives and you may find that this is just not the right route for you, which is fine. For example, if you have an addictive personality and don't know when to quit when you are ahead, binary options may not be the right one for you. This investment choice is for those with level heads and those who deal with addictive personalities can quickly start to lose their rationale during these situations.

In addition, if you are someone who gets stressed out pretty easily or are considering using some money that you just can't lose, like money on your house, this is not the investment opportunity for you. Binary options are high risk and you can just as easily lose money as you can make money. Those who are new to the market, can't control their thinking and emotions in high risk situations, and those who don't like the idea of possibility losing money need to pick another option.

The Differences with Binary Options

Many people get binary options confused with forex trading. These are two very different kinds of investment options even though they may seem to share a few similarities. If you are going into binary options simply because you understand forex trading or you have done this in the past, you could end up in a lot of trouble.

Before going into binary trading, make sure you understand all the differences that occur between this investment and other options like forex trading. You want to understand all the rules of the game so you have the best chance of winning. In addition, find a good broker, someone who will work with clients from your area and who will really treat you well in the process. There are some brokers who are just interested in making money and don't care much for their customers; don't get stuck with one of these individuals because they can make your money disappear quickly.

Pick out a good company to work with and get some of your tools in place. A good graphing website or another location to keep track of your options can be helpful. This can give you a chance to glance over how the option is doing and see if you need to make any changes. Learn how these programs work or have frequent meetings with your advisor to make sure you are on the right track.

Binary options can be a confusing to someone who may be new to the investment scene. It is often not the investment choice that you will start out with as there are high risks, it can sometimes cause confusion, and the investment is not the type everyone will like. But for those who are able to understand how the market works, are willing to take some big risks, and who have been in the investment world for some time, binary options can be the new choice you have been looking for.

Chapter 2: Tools That You Need as a Binary Trader

Before you get started with binary options, you may find that having a few tools around can make all of the difference. These tools are going to help you keep track of the different investments that you are using and can make it easier to tell when one is doing well and another may need a bit of help. Some of the tools that you can find useful with your binary options include:

Chart Pattern Tools

One of the most important tools that you can bring into your strategy is the chart pattern recognition tool. These charts are going to be able to show the direction that the asset is taking, or has been taking over time. In a trading world where your success hinges on how well a certain asset is doing, it can be nice to see where that asset has gone in the past so you can make the right prediction.

Say someone comes up to you, talking about how this currency is doing so well and you should get into binary options by predicting that it goes up. There are many brokers who are in this industry who would love for you to jump on a currency and get rich and they will try to help you out. But there are also lots of others who would just like to get the fees from you, regardless of whether or not you see success with that particular option. They may be good sales people who can get you all revved up about an option without ever showing you a single thing about it.

As a smart investor, you should know that it takes some research to really know whether an option is a good one or not. Just taking someone's word for it can get you in some trouble. This is where the chart pattern tool can come in handy. You can look up the option that you are interested in and see where it is going. If you notice that there has been a downward trend on the option for some time now, it is probably not a good idea to jump in and put all your money on it, no matter how good of a speaker that broker was.

In addition, once you place your prediction on a binary option, it is a good idea to track where it is going, especially if you plan to follow it for the next few years before seeing the results. One of these charting pattern tools can make this easier by providing you with information on how the option is doing from month to month or even each day.

The Autopivot Calculator

This kind of calculator is going to work by using the previous days' closing prices, low, and high. These calculators are often free online and you will be able to create your own to go with any graph that you want, in order to get the best results and see where your options are going. You will be able to use the closing, high, and low of the option and get a clear picture of how the option is going to be doing.

With this calculator, you are going to get a better idea of whether this is a good option to go with. it is going to show you where this option should land based on the current market conditions and where your option is right now. You will be able to use it to make your predictions and hopefully come out ahead. Look online to find an autopivot calculator that you like and mess around with it a little bit to learn how it works.

Charts

Never go into your binary option trading without having some charts available. Without the charts, you are basically going into this process blind and hoping you come out a millionaire. Despite what you may hear from some of the "best" in the industry, this is not a good idea and you need to have a wide variety of charts available before you can see success with binary options.

Charts allow you to get some of the technical analysis that you need in order to see, in a pictorial reference, what is going on with the market. So before getting too far into your trading, find a good source for interactive charts that can make this process easier. MT4 is a good place to start because it is going to show you mostly the same assets that are traded on the binary options market. A broker may be able to provide you with one of these charts as well.

You can then follow the charts for some time to see how the different options are doing and whether they are the right one for you.

Demo Accounts

As someone who is new to the market, it can be nice to have a demo account to help you out. This is like a practice round, where you can put different numbers in place and see how the market is going to react, how things are expected to change, and then you can make the changes you see fit as time goes on. You can make mistakes without having to put any money into the market, and you can really learn how this whole process works.

There are a few companies that do allow this, but be careful. Most brokers are not in the business of handing out free stuff and if you are just allowed to play all the time and never invest, they are not going to make any money. Most brokers won't offer this service, though it can help to limit your fears about binary options, and those that do offer this service will put limitations on the amount of time that you are able to use it.

Despite this, if you are able to find a way to use a demo account, even if it's just for a short little bit, go ahead and try it out. This can help you understand the market a little bit better before putting your money into it and going blind. If your broker will work with you and provides a demo account to you, this is something that you should give a try to make sure that you are ready to go.

Chapter 3: Types of Binary Options

The next thing that you should concentrate on is choosing the type of binary option that you would like to work with. As a beginner trader, you may want to just stick with one type of binary option so you can start to understand the market and get a handle on everything. As you get more experience with this kind of investing, you can add several different types together in order to diversify your portfolio. Some of the most common types of binary options that you can choose includes:

Digital Option

This is the most common type of binary option and it goes by several different names including CALL/PUT option and UP/DOWN Option. With this option, you are going to place a CALL if you believe the price is going to end higher than the entry price after a certain set time. You will use a PUT if you believe the price is going to go down.

So you are basically going to determine whether the price is going to go up or down after you place your entry. You can choose between the different lengths that you would like to wait and then make your predictions. For example, if you think that the price is going to go up by the end of the day, you will place a CALL on it. If the price does end up going up by the end of the day, you would receive a percentage of the profit when it closes. The same would happen if you thought the price would go down and it does.

On the other hand, if you predict incorrectly, you can lose your money based on a percentage that is determined from the beginning. This is why there is such a risk with this kind of trading; there is a 50 percent chance that you are going to be wrong and could lose all the money that you invest in just a few short minutes.

There are a variety of expiry periods on this kind of trading ranging from sixty seconds to the end of the day. Once you have placed your prediction and committed to the trade, the platform is going to monitor the trade and will exit you at the time you appointed. You don't need to log into the system and there is no additional work as you just need to sit back and watch what is going on. At the closing of each of your trades, the system will send you an email about the status for you to check on.

Touch Option

The next option that you can choose is the Touch option. There are a few varieties including Touch, Double Touch, and No Touch. This option is going to come with rates that are predefined in order to win the trade, and includes a bit more work rather than just predicting whether the value of the asset is going to decrease or increase. In this kind of trading, you have to be able to predict at which level it will reach or not reach.

This one can be a bit trickier. You not only have to decide if the value is going to decrease or increase, but you have to predict how high or low the value will go. This can take a bit more, but offers a bit better return on investment if you do well.

This option can be purchased over the weekend while the markets are closed. Over the next week, the trades will occur and once the asset touches or surpasses the level determined over the weekend, the system will declare you as a winner. You can then receive your payout, even if it reaches this value on Monday. You are basically going to get five days and five chances to hit this target though as the platform is going to continue checking each day until Friday.

No touch is going to be paid out when the level that is defined is never reached and Double touch is when either of the levels are reached. For most traders, one touch is ideal because you only have to reach the predetermined level once rather than having it stay there for the long term, making it easier to deal with the volatile market.

60 Second Option

The 60 second option is gaining in popularity, even though you will have to be careful with this option since it can quickly change. But a lot of traders like this option because you can check the asset and if it has a clear trend of going up, you can quickly make some money by trading a few times in the next few minutes. If you are excited for some quick rewards, want to get a feel for the market, and have a bit of money to grow, this can be a great option. Just be careful and pick options that aren't going to take nose dive and lose all your money.

Boundary Options

Next on the list is boundary options or tunnel options. This one is similar to the touch option, but there are going to be two defined levels. Upper and lower levels will be defined, or the range and boundary, and the trader will need the asset to be somewhere inside this boundary in order to get their payout. There are some brokers who will allow trades for the payout if it does go outside the boundary.

So you will pick a range where you think that this option is going to be for a set amount of time. As long as the option stays in this range, you will receive a payout at the end of the week. But if it goes out of the range (unless you have another agreement with the broker), you will lose your money.

This is the option that you should go with if the market is pretty stable. If the market is going all over the place, it is going to be hard to keep it within a certain range. But a steady market can help you to keep it within this range and makes it more likely that you will get your money at the end.

Other Options

Depending on the broker you are working with, there may be some other options that you can choose. Some will allow you to make a trade right in the middle of the set time, some will offer different analytic tools, and so on. You should shop around and see which options are available for your needs so you can make a profit and not lose it all.

As you can see, all of these options for trading have some different rules that go along with them. Some are a bit easier to handle and others require you to really know the market in order to succeed. Investigate all of the options, find a good broker, and you are sure to see success as you learn more about binary options over time.

Chapter 4: The Different Trading Times and Lengths

When you are getting started with trading, you want to make sure to figure out the best times and lengths of trading that you should do to make the most out of your money. Knowing why and how the market is moving will be important if you are looking to make money with this option. You also need to know when the different currencies are going to make the biggest moves. While this kind of trading can be done five and a half days a week for twenty-four hours a day, there are some hours that are going to be a bit better than others.

One strategy that you can try is to trade when two markets are overlapping. These are times when there will be the highest volume, as well as volatility, with trading so you are going to get some better prices on your options. Some prices to keep track of include:

- The Asian Session—6 p.m. to 3 a.m. EST.
- The European Session (London)—2 a.m. to 11 a.m. EST
- The North American Session—7 a.m. to 3 p.m. EST.

As you can see, there are a few times when these are going to overlap, making them better times to trade and get some good prices. This is also why there isn't always a lot of activity with the New York stock exchange until 9:30 in the morning since the other time areas aren't doing much action either.

A good habit that you can develop is to check the news announcements that are out and will affect you at the time you are trading. If there are some announcements during these times, you should also check to see which currencies it is affecting. This can make a big difference on how well your options are doing.

The news releases that you should pay attention to including interest rate changes, housing sales, and unemployment rates that are released from the governments across the world. These are big events that are going to change how strong or weak the currency is and can help to determine how much the option will be worth

If you plan to do your trading during the different sessions, there are a few basics that you need to know. First, you need to get a good understanding of what currency pairs are going to move the most and at what times these changes are going to occur. For example, the North American sessions are going to have the most movement with pairs that have either CAD and USD most of the time. On the other hand, the Asian session will have the most price action with pairs of AUD or JPY and the European Session is going to have price action with pairs that include GBP and EUR.

Look for these pairs based on the session that you are trading in. If you are smart about the trading, you will want to make sure the right pairs are showing up if you would like to see a big profit.

Another thing that you should take note of is that each session will behave in a different matter. For examples, the New York session in North America has wild fluctuations with prices that will move around quite a bit. If you like the opportunity to see a lot of movement with your options, this is the one to trade within. On the other hand, some people are not that happy with all the fluctuations that come with the North American Session and will go with the Asian Session since it is a bit calmer. You should take a look at all the different sessions and then find which one is best for your personal investing style.

Best (and Worst) Lengths for Trading

One thing that draws a lot of people to binary options is seeing how some people are able to grow their bank accounts overnight. Brokers have a lot of options when it comes to trading these options, from thirty second trading to end of the day and so much in between. If you are seeing a promotional video about binary options and someone is claiming how quick it is to make money, you are most likely seeing a one-minute trade.

Keep in mind that these are meant to get you excited and while you may be able to make some higher amounts of money with this option, it also comes with a high risk. With a one-minute trading option, you are trying to determine what a currency is going to do in the next minute and if it will make you a profit. This is hard to foresee because currencies are always moving and go up and down all the time. It is always easier to make this prediction in an hour, day, or even longer, which is why there is a higher risk with one-minute trading.

As a beginner, it is often not the best to choose trading on a one-minute option. These are really volatile and you could end up losing a lot of money in just a minute if you don't know what you are doing. But if you are considering going into the market, looking at one-minute trading charts can help you to make some decisions about your trading and can be used for long term forecasting. While it can be helpful, it is not a good idea to get started with this kind of trading.

Going for longer times is a bit easier to go with. You won't have to worry so much about the volatility of the market quite so much and will have a bit more time to determine the patterns that are showing up with your particular option. Make sure that you study the options before getting started to see if they look like smart investments

As you can see, this is not always an easy process. There are many time lengths that you can worry about and understanding how each of them will work for you is not always easy. Finding a good broker can make a big difference in how well you do. They will be able to discuss the options, show you the trends, and make sure that you are picking something that is best for your financial goals.

Chapter 5: Understanding Brokers and How They Influence Trading

At this point, you are probably excited about getting started with binary options. You may have saved up a little bit of money and want to get into the game to try your hand out with it. But before you can go any further, you need to make sure that you are finding the right broker to help you get this done.

The broker is going to be your primary point of contact with this. They are the company that you work with when choosing your asset and making the trades. Even though binary options are a relatively new way of investing, there are hundreds of brokers who work in this field and all of them are going to be fighting to get your business. All this competition can be good for you as it gives you more options for your investment, but how do you pick out the right broker for you?

Part of your winning strategy is going to be choosing the right broker for your binary options. And while there are a lot of great talkers out there who will make big promises and who may try to convince you to just hand over the money and let them do the work, remember that you are always the one in charge. If you don't like a broker, even if they are said to be one of the best in the world, you do not have to stay with them. Another option is to choose to go with two or more brokers at the same time so that you have a lot of diversity and don't have to rely on just one person or company to make the money.

So how do you find the right broker to make you the money. First, you need to go through some online reviews. You want to find a broker who has a good working relationship with the other customers they have had. You want to go with someone who has a lot of reviews because this shows that the company has been in business for a long time and knows what they are doing.

Then take some time to read through the reviews. You want complete reviews written about the companies you are considering, all of the top brokers in binary options will have reputable and legal reviews written about them. So go through and see what the official reviews are for what the company offers, how long they have been in business, and so on. But also read some of the customer reviews. Are other customers satisfied with the services and bonuses they receive from the company? Are there a lot of negative reviews that make the company seem shady and unprofessional that you should be worried bout?

While researching the broker options, take a look at their professional history. Have they been in business for a long time and have a good reputation? Do they have the right certificates that are required in your state for performing binary options? Do they have a good history of providing good customer service, helping their clients to succeed, and avoiding poor money management that would purposely make the customers lose money? Make sure you are able to answer all of these questions before choosing a company.

In addition to making sure that a broker is legitimate and won't just steal your money, take a time to make sure that the company is the right fit for you. For example, are they going to accept the form of payment that works for you such as cash, credit card, or check? Have you tried out their system and find that it is easy to navigate or use or is it just too difficult for you to make sense of? Does the platform work on your personal computer? It doesn't make sense to go with a broker that doesn't work with your needs.

Each broker company is going to offer different assets to the clients and this is going to be important when choosing a broker as well as how much of a percentage you can earn on the options. For example, if you want to work with Asian currencies, you want to pick a company that has many options of currencies in this form. Some brokers may focus just on stocks and only have two options in Asian currencies. The broker may be amazing, but since they don't specialize in what you need, you may have to choose someone else.

Once you find a few brokers who are reputable and have the assets that you are looking for, you should focus on finding out which one has the best percentage returns. This can make a big difference on how much you are able to make from your investments. Something as small as just one percent can actually mean thousands of extra dollars over the long term. If everything else is equal, you should go with the broker that has the highest percentage return.

Of course, there are times when one broker may offer a higher percentage in one asset while another offers a higher percentage in something else. It is perfectly fine to have two or more brokers that cover each of your assets. This is actually smart since you won't have to rely on just one company to make your fortune (so if something goes wrong you won't lose all your money) and you can get the most return of investment with higher percentages across the board.

While looking at the assets and percentages, check to see if the broker offers any rebates on losing trades. This is a good protection option that can help to keep the portfolio profitable when short term downturns occurred. Some will offer up to fifteen percent on any trades that lose, which helps to lower the risk, but keep in mind that not all brokers are going to offer this protection.

Bonuses are always a good perk to look for. As mentioned, there is a lot of competition when it comes to finding a good binary options broker and the different companies are going to use different options and bonuses to try and convince you to use them instead of another company. One option to look for is whether the broker will offer you a bonus when you sign up and make your first deposit. You should never choose a broker just because they offer this bonus, but it can be a nice addition to make your money go further when you first start out.

By this point, you have most likely limited your options to just a few brokers you would like to use and are ready to sign up. Remember that if at any time you are working with a broker and you don't like how they are managing things or feel someone else would be a better fit, don't be afraid to make a change. You are the one in charge of your money and if you don't like how things are going, it is up to you to make those changes. You are in full control of your investment and your money so don't let the broker make you feel uncomfortable or try to make you do what isn't in your best interests.

Picking out a broker for binary options is really important. They are the ones who offer you all the options, the bonuses, the assets, and so much more. If you pick the wrong company, you could end up with a lot of money lost or lower gains than another company could offer. On the other hand, if you choose a good company with a great reputation, good customer service, and lots of bonuses and assets, you are well on your way to make a good income with investing in binary options.

Chapter 6: Picking Your Strategy for Success

When you first get into binary options, you want to make sure you pick a strategy that will help you to win. It is never a good idea to pick the first asset on the list and then see how it goes. You may end up with something that loses you a lot of money. Instead, you need to understand how the market works, pick out an asset that interests you and has a good history, and figure out the winning strategy that makes you comfortable and will allow you to come out ahead on most of your deals.

There are a lot of different strategies that you can use with binary options and each of them have different things you will look at. None of them are necessarily better than the others so it is often a matter of preference for which one you choose. When you are just starting out, consider these great strategies, and perhaps try a mixture of them, to come up with your game winning plan.

Technical Analysis

The first strategy we will look at is technical, or chart, analysis. For this strategy, you will need to take a look at the charts for exchange rates of the different assets with a particular broker. While you may not go with all of these assets, this is going to give you a better understanding of the current market and where it may be going in the future.

Many assets follow the idea of "market remembers." Just like the idea that history repeats itself, it seems that many assets have the same kind of thing. If you look over the long term with the market and various assets, you will see that there are trends that like to repeat themselves over time. If you noticed that every two years a particular asset has a downward turn and it has been about two years since the last downward turn, you may want to predict that the asset is going to go down in order to win.

While it may take some time to understand how the charts work and what they are telling you, this can be a very good indicator, especially if you are doing binary options over the long term. It may not be the best for sixty second trading because you never know what is going to happen from day to day, it can work well if you want to follow the trends over weeks or months because these same trends are likely to repeat themselves.

Traders' Tendency Indicator

Another strategy that you can try is to look at the indicator of traders' tendency which your online broker can provide to you. This is a tool that is going to describe the balance of positions during a purchase and then a sale of each asset at any given moment. When the broker provides you with this information, it is going to show how many clients are in position to purchase, based on a percentage, and the amount of clients who are in a position to sale on a certain asset.

This one is kind of hard to use though. Since the clients of online brokers are not able to trade on Wall Street, even though some of them do, this tool can become obsolete unless you really know how to make the market work and have worked with binary options and stocks in the past. Be careful with this option and perhaps choose one of the others since it has a high failure rate.

Fundamental Analysis

Fundamental analysis is going to focus on statistics that concern the economy and will take a look at the economic climate overall in order to predict how the exchange rate is going to change. This can take some research and you will really need to look at a lot of different news sources to figure out the right way to predict in these cases, but it can be highly effective. For example, those who were paying attention in early 2008 were able to predict that the economy was going to go down and therefor placed a stake in the assets going down. They came out big while others who may have been new to the game would stake upwards, assuming the economy would continue to go up.

While 2008 is a big event that occurred and helped to make and ruin lots of investors, there are some smaller scale indicators of the economy that are published each day and may include the unemployment rates for each country. These can be shown in real time and will help you to recognize patterns and make more educated predictions if you are paying attention.

Martingale Type Betting

First, martingale is a method of betting where the better, or you, is going to increase how much you invest initially after every loss until you achieve a gain. For example, if you place $20 in the exchange rate going up and then it ends up going down. Then the next time you place a bet you would make your prediction and put up $40 or some other amount. The idea behind this is that after a few losses, you are going to win and you can make back any of the money that you lost along the way.

This can be a really tricky way to go, especially in the beginning when you aren't sure how this process goes. It can also be dangerous if you have an addictive personality and you don't know when to quit. While this method is going to help you get your money back and even get ahead if you just suffer from a few losses in a row, if you start to lose for a very long time, you could lose thousands of dollars and run out of money.

Basically, unless you have a lot of money that you are willing to lose and you are willing to ride this thing out, the martingale type betting is not the best way to win it big in binary options.

Minimizing Your Risks

The most important thing that you can do when working with binary options is to learn how to minimize your risks. While there is always going to be some risk with doing this kind of investing, as with any kind of investing, there are steps that you can take to ensure that you are not going to lose out on everything each time that you make a prediction. Some of the things that you can do to help minimize your risks with binary options include:

Picking out a good broker
The broker you choose to go with is going to be a big influence on the assets you can work with, any bonuses you get, and even whether you get a discount when you predict incorrectly on a particular asset. You should take a look at what each broker has to offer, and even spread out your assets among several different assets to ensure that you are avoiding risks and getting the biggest return possible.

Never go with the first broker who comes your way. While they may be amazing and one of the best, it is still a good idea to do some research and find one who is going to have your best interests at hand. And it is never a bad idea to separate out your money between two or more brokers; this can help to limit the risk and will help you to get the best rates on each asset you want to use.

Doing your research

It is never a good idea to go into binary options without doing some research. Each asset is going to react to things differently and while they often follow the same trend as the current economy, some do go off on their own or are affected by some outside factors. You need to do your research and talk to other investors, look at news information, and look over charts before deciding to put your money into any asset.

When you first sit down with a broker, consider asking for some charts and information to determine how each asset is going to do. You can also talk to your representative in the broker and find out how each asset has been doing, what seems to be popular with other clients, and any other information that you can find out. This process may take a bit longer, but it is going to make a world of difference in helping you to choose the right asset and in ensuring you get a great return on investment.

Separating out your assets

Never choose to put all of your available money into one asset. This may seem like a good way to increase your money quickly, but it is also a good way to lose your money in no time at all. It is always best to separate your money out in between at least two different options if not more. Some of the most successful investors choose to only invest five percent of their money into each asset or option.

This may seem like a little bit of an overkill, but it is actually really smart. When you put all of your money into one asset, you are increasing your risk. If the asset does well, you will do well but if the asset starts to do poorly, you could lose everything. On the other hand, when you separate out your money between different options, one can start to fail a bit and you only lose a bit of money rather than the whole thing. But if the market is doing well, you still have a chance to see an increase in all of your money.

26

Take the time to look at all the different assets that are available, even among the different brokers. Pick at least a couple different assets you would like to follow, and even different lengths of time you would like to follow them, to diversify your portfolio. This may take a bit more work, but you are going to find that the risk goes way down and you can still see a huge profit in the long run.

Picking a good strategy for binary options is one of the most important things that you can do to see success. This strategy is going to determine how you go about your investing, ensures that you stay on a track that is comfortable for you, and that you actually spend most of your time seeing wins rather than losses. Consider one of these strategies to help you see positive results with this investment.

Chapter 7: Being Scammed—How to Avoid

As you go through this process, you may notice that there are a lot of scammers out there. Websites are popping up all over, claiming to be brokers who can give you a great return on your investment and make promises that are too good to be true. Some of these scams are going to be pretty obvious; just one look at their website and reading a few reviews will tell you that they are someone you shouldn't work with. But there are some that are a bit harder to notice. Thanks to the ability to receive high profits and many inexperienced investors who just want to make a quick buck, binary options scammers are all over the place.

This does not mean you are not able to protect yourself. Being a smart consumer and watching out for these common signs can help you to find the right broker without having someone take all of your hard earned money for free. Some of the signs you should watch out for to avoid being scammed with binary options include:

- Look for a free demo—take a look at brokers that offer that free demo account. This is a great way not only for you to learn a bit more about how the broker works and how to do binary options, but it is going to exploit the scams right away.
- High payouts—if you are talking to a broker and they seem to offer really high return rates (like much higher than any other broker is offering), you are probably dealing with a scam. Most reputable brokers are going to offer between 68 and 90 percent returns on any winning trade. If a broker is offering above this, you may want to take a closer look before you submit a deposit. They are either making claims that they can't keep or they are a scam.

- Bonus incentives—be careful with the bonus incentives. While many brokers offer these in order to convince you to go with them rather than any one else, scammers are going to take advantage of this as well. You need to read the fine print first. Yes, the scam may offer to give you a bonus of your deposit, but if you need to generate a volume of trades that forty times your original deposit amount, it is unlikely that you will ever get that money back.

- Fine print—there is always fine print with any company you choose to go with, but scammers are able to hide a lot of information in fine print that no one wants to read. If you read through all of this, you may notice the higher fees you have to pay, the issues with the bonus incentive, and so much more. Always read the fine print and find out if something seems off.

- Website look—when you go onto the brokers website, does something seem a little bit off? A professional broker is going to have a nice professional website, one that is easy to use, has all the information up front, and even has the option to try out a demo of the site. On the other hand, a scammer is going to hide as much information as possible and often wastes valuable space just talking about how much you will be able to make with them.

- Funding options—reputable brokers are going to offer you a variety of payment options to best fit your needs. For example, they may offer an online payment processor, bank transfers, and credit and debit cards. There are not going to be any issues with making your deposit and when you are ready to withdraw your profits, you are sure to be in good hands. On the other hand, if the website has lots of holds on your withdrawals, only accepts one type of payment (Western Union anyone?) and just makes things difficult, you can just kiss that deposit goodbye.

Your goal as a trader should be to work with a broker who is respected and trustworthy. With the right company, you are going to have a lot of options and a fair chance of making a profit as long as you make good predictions and know how the system works. You won't have to worry about the deposits that you are making getting "lost" and the withdrawal process being too difficult. Honest and reputable brokers are going to make money when you do and they want to see you succeed. A scammer is just going to be interested in taking your money and running away without doing the work. Learn how to spot a scammer and how to avoid them, and trading in binary options can become so much easier.

Chapter 8: Tips to Succeed in Binary Options

The idea behind binary options seems simple. You choose an asset that is in the market and make a prediction about whether it will finish lower or higher than the starting price when you trade it later on. If you are right, you can make money but if you are wrong, you could lose out on a lot of money as well. There is a lot of risk that comes with binary options, but for those who understand the market and can think clearly this is a great way to make a lot of money.

If you are thinking about getting started with binary options and want to make sure that you are doing everything that you can in order to see success, follow these simple tips to make it a reality!

- Understand your trading tools and the market—you can not just jump into this game and expect to win out big. This makes investing a gamble, something that you can quickly lose at. Instead, learn what tools are at your disposal and take some time to learn about the market, and you stand a better chance of doing a good job.
- Choose the right broker—there are many great brokers in binary options, but there are also plenty of brokers who don't care about you and just want to make money. So make sure to fully research the broker you want to use, try out their demo system, and ask questions to ensure that the broker has a good reputation and you aren't losing money because of their poor money management.
- Learn the process of trading—this may be an obvious point, but if you don't understand the basics of trading with binary options, it is going to be really hard to make good predictions and make a profit. Make sure you research the trading process so you can see success.

- Implement your strategy—before starting, you need to pick out your strategy. Do you want to take on more risk to make more money or would you like something that is a bit safer? Do you want to make the length longer or go with minute by minute trading? Your strategy will depend with what you want out of the process as well as the market so determine this right from the beginning and to ensure that you don't go off track.

- Choose your assets wisely—picking a rare or non-common asset may seem like the best choice, but you are going to have trouble finding analysis about these assets and you may have limited options for trading that asset. Go with those that are common, those that have a lot of news and analysis so you can see how things have changed so you can make informed decisions.

- Try out a demo system—this is one of the best things that you can do. Understanding how binary options work can be a challenge, but these demo systems can help you to see how binary options work, how different decisions will affect your money, and so on. Some brokers will offer a demo system, though they are often for limited times. Take advantage of this to ensure you understand this investing option before sinking your money in.

- Manage the risks—putting all your money into one binary option method is a bad idea. This is a lot of risk to put into one trade so if you want to make this your primary investment option, learn how to separate out the risk. Try a few different binary options or break it up between binary options and other investment options so you don't have as high of risk.

- One-hour binary options—really long term binary options can be tricky. You never know what a market is going to do over time. On the other hand, one-minute options can make you lose money quickly as well. One-hour binary options seem to be a good option to go with because it allows for some variation but is still short enough to estimate well. It is also a quick way to make some profit and can increase your confidence as a newbie.

- Have binary option signals sent to you—these signal provides can issue predictions right to your email on a regular basis. If the provider has a high ratio of winning, they have probably done a lot of analysis and research before releasing the signal and they can be a good one to go with. Of course, these signals aren't always correct, but they can lead you in the right direction.

- This is not a get rich quick option—some traders get into binary options because they feel it is a way to make a lot of money really quickly. While this can sometimes happen, you have to realize that this also means you can lose money quickly. You need to be realistic and take caution with binary options, rather than losing your head, and you may start to see some good results in your pocketbook over time.

Going with binary options can be a great investment opportunity. They provide you with an option to make some decent money in real time and much faster compared to other investment opportunities. With that being said, it is also possible to lose money a lot faster than other investment opportunities so you need to be careful. Follow some of these tips and you may find that binary options will work for you!

Conclusion

When it comes to finding the right investment option for your financial security, there are a lot of choices. Some people choose to go with putting their money in a safe retirement plan and adding a savings account to have money for later on. Others may go into real estate or the stock market to have some more active control in the money they make and to enjoy the income now rather than working their regular nine to five jobs.

Another option for investing that we explore in this guidebook is binary options. This is a great way to make money relatively quickly, but you need to have a clear and level head and understand how the market works. You can choose between a variety of options including one-minute, one hour, and even day long options of predicting to make a good sum of money quickly. While the process sounds simple though, there are a lot of intricacies that you will have to work with and the risk is high with this kind of investing.

If you are considering going into binary options and are unsure of where to start, this guidebook has the answers that you need. We spent some time discussing what binary options are, the different options that you have with binary options, how to make the market work for you, and even how to find the right broker to make it successful. Don't go in the dark and try to make this investment opportunity work for you, use the tips and tricks in this guidebook to really see success.

Made in the USA
Middletown, DE
26 September 2022

11303244R00022